Foreword

Welcome to God's home! You thought his home was in heaven Well, that's one of his homes, but he has many homes here on earth. The closest one to you may be a Catholic church. A Catholic church is a special place. You may visit it every Sunday or Saturday evening when you attend weekly Mass. You were probably there at other times: receiving the sacrament of Baptism, seeking forgiveness of sins in the sacrament of Reconciliation, or participating in a prayer service.

Perhaps you also made a visit in the middle of the day when no ceremony was taking place. You may have gone to church just to sit and pray. In this quiet place you shared with God your joys and sorrows, your fears and certainties, your hopes and your disappointments. In the quiet of God's home, God may have spoken to you and told you not to be afraid or showed you how to overcome an obstacle.

Because a Catholic church is such a special place, you'll want to know all about it. The parts of a Catholic church should not be unknown to you, because lack of knowledge sometimes results in fear. Our God is a loving God. He wants his children not to fear him but to love him.

Father Michael Keane, with the help of photographer Aaron Pepis, has created this beautiful book to help you understand what is in a Catholic church. Take the book with you the next time you visit a church and compare the pictures in the book with what you see in your church. Read the text to discover what an altar is, why there are candles and flowers, why there are statues and stained glass windows, and many other items. After having done this you will feel very comfortable in God's home—and this is what God wants.

Robert J. Kealey, Ed.D.
Executive Director,
Department of Elementary Schools,
National Catholic Educational Association

What You Will See Inside
A CATHOLIC CHURCH

Reverend Michael Keane
Photographs by Aaron Pepis

Walking Together, Finding the Way
SKYLIGHT PATHS Publishing
Woodstock, Vermont

This book is dedicated to my mom and dad, who were the first to bring me inside a Catholic church on the day of my baptism. I thank them for the gift of faith, which they shared with me as a child. It was planted by their love and watered by their example. I also dedicate this work to my nieces, nephew, and godchildren. I pray that Sarah, Melissa, Lauren, Anna, Anthony, Grace, Erin, Zachary, and Jade will visit God's house often and find within it a sense of welcome, warmth, and wonder. —Reverend Michael Keane

SkyLight Paths Publishing extends appreciation to the Roman Catholic churches in the Archdiocese of New York, who generously allowed us to photograph their church interiors:

Church of the Holy Name of Mary, Croton-on-Hudson; Church of St. Anthony, Nanuet; Church of St. Columba, Hopewell Junction; Church of Saint Joseph, Poughkeepsie; Church of St. Martin de Porres, Poughkeepsie; Our Lady of the Rosary Chapel of St. Peter's Church, Poughkeepsie; St. Ann's Church, Nyack; St. Francis of Assisi Church, West Nyack; St. Gregory Barbarigo Church, Garnerville; Saint Pius X Church, Scarsdale.

SkyLight Paths Publishing is creating a place where people of different spiritual traditions come together for challenge and inspiration, a place where we can help each other understand the mystery that lies at the heart of our existence.

SkyLight Paths sees both believers and seekers as a community that increasingly transcends traditional boundaries of religion and denomination—people wanting to learn from each other, *walking together, finding a way.*

What You Will See Inside a Catholic Church

Nihil Obstat: William B. Smith, S.T.D., Censor Librorum
Imprimatur: † Robert A. Brucato, D.D., Vicar General, Archdiocese of New York

Text © 2002 by Michael Keane
Illustrations © 2002 by the Pepis Studio

Library of Congress Cataloging-in-Publication Data
Keane, Michael, 1961–
What you will see inside a Catholic Church / Michael Keane ; photographs by Aaron Pepis.
   p. cm. — (What you will see inside—)
Summary: Names and explains the various objects found in a Catholic Church, how they are used in the celebration of the Mass and other events, the clergy and lay people who use them, and the meaning behind them.
ISBN 1-893361-54-3 (hardcover)
1. Mass—Juvenile literature. 2. Church year—Juvenile literature. 3. Sacraments—Catholic Church—Juvenile literature. 4. Catholic Church—Liturgical objects—Juvenile literature. [1. Mass. 2. Catholic Church. 3. Sacraments—Catholic Church. 4. Church year.] I. Pepis, Aaron, ill. II. Title. III. Series.
BX2230.3 .K43 2002
264'.02—dc21
                                                                                                        2002008077

10 9 8 7 6 5 4 3 2 1

Manufactured in Malaysia
Book and Jacket design: Dawn DeVries Sokol

SkyLight Paths, "Walking Together, Finding the Way" and colophon are trademarks of LongHill Partners, Inc., registered in the U.S. Patent and Trademark Office.

Walking Together, Finding the Way
Published by SkyLight Paths Publishing
A Division of LongHill Partners, Inc.
Sunset Farm Offices, Route 4, P.O. Box 237
Woodstock, VT 05091
Tel: (802) 457-4000   Fax: (802) 457-4004
www.skylightpaths.com

A Special Message to Young People

Catholic churches are a lot like God's people—we don't all look the same. That's what makes us so special. We are unique individuals created by God. Churches are special buildings created by people. Just like God's people, some churches are old and some are young. Some are dark on the outside and some are light. Some are large, like cathedrals, and some are small, like chapels. Even though churches may look different on the outside, inside they contain the same important things. Just like us!

All Catholic churches contain Tabernacles where the Blessed Sacrament is kept. They all have altars where the holy sacrifice of the Mass is offered, and lecterns where the word of God is proclaimed. But most important, all churches have people who come to pray and make up the community of faith.

Introduction

WELCOME! COME IN! Make yourself at home! It's always good to visit the home of a family member or friend and celebrate our time together. We might share stories with one another about important people and events in our lives. We might sit down at a table and enjoy a wonderful meal together. We might sing songs together. It's good just to be with people we love.

Going to God's house is just like visiting a person who loves us. At church we hear stories about God and God's people from the Bible. In the Catholic Church we share a meal called the Eucharist. We sing songs together in God's house, too!

So let's open the door to a Catholic church and look at some of the wonderful things we will find there.

Welcome to the Altar

"THE LORD BE WITH YOU." This is the greeting that the priest uses to welcome the people to church. It reminds us that God is with us when we pray together.

EUCHARIST: The sacrament in which the people gather to celebrate and remember the death and resurrection of Jesus. It is also the name of the Body and Blood of Jesus Christ that we receive at Mass.

The altar is a very special table that is found in all Catholic churches. The altar is the place where the priest offers the bread and wine to God. After the bread and wine are consecrated, they become the Body and Blood of Jesus Christ, known as the Eucharist. This happens when God's people gather in church for a celebration that is called the Mass.

PRESIDER'S CHAIR: The chair that the priest sits in at Mass when he is not standing at the altar. The altar servers' chairs are next to the presider's chair.

PROCESSIONAL CROSS: The cross that is carried into the church when Mass begins. It reminds us to be thankful that Jesus died for our sins.

PRIEST: A man who receives the sacrament of Holy Orders. He leads God's people in prayer, celebrates the sacraments with them, and serves them in the name of Jesus.

The picture on this altar shows the Last Supper that Jesus had with his closest friends, who are known as the Apostles. Jesus gave his Apostles the gift of the Eucharist at that supper. Today we still celebrate the Eucharist around the altar in church.

Altar servers are boys and girls who help the priest during Mass. They sometimes carry the cross and candles and help prepare the altar during Mass.

The place at the front of the church where the altar is found is called the sanctuary. The word *sanctuary* means "holy place." It is the place where we proclaim God's word and welcome Jesus to our altar.

We Gather Together

WHEN GOD'S PEOPLE GATHER to celebrate the Eucharist, they are called a congregation. The special wooden benches where people sit in church are called pews. Everyone faces toward the priest at the altar. During the readings and some of the prayers, the congregation sits. But when the Gospel is read from one of the first four books of the New Testament, all the people stand. And everyone kneels during the most holy part of the

KNEELER: A soft padded fold-down bench that is attached to the pews, used for kneeling in prayer.

ARCHES: Traditional high, pointed doorways or roofs that remind us of the shape of praying hands, sending our prayers up to God.

Mass, when Jesus becomes present on our altar in the Eucharist.

When you go to a church, you will see people praying in different ways. Some people close their eyes, some bow their heads, and some put their hands together pointing up to God.

Catholic churches are built in the shape of a cross to remind us that Jesus died for our sins. The altar and sanctuary are at the top of the cross. The ceilings and roofs of many churches have high arches that point upward to heaven. This reminds us that our prayers and praise are going up to God.

PEWS: The long benches where the people sit during Mass. Some pews have comfortable cushions on the seats. Every pew has a place to hold hymnbooks and missalettes, which are booklets that give us the words and readings used in each day's Mass.

Hearing God's Words

EVERYBODY LOVES GOOD STORIES. The Bible is God's word given to us. It is filled with stories about God's people.

The person who proclaims the readings during Mass is called a lector. The lector might be a man, a woman, or even a young person. The lector reads from a book called a lectionary. The lectionary contains stories, poems, songs, and letters from the Bible. Some lectionaries have beautiful gold covers and pages. That shows how important and valuable the words inside are to us.

The special stand from which the lector reads God's word is called a lectern. Many lecterns are beautifully made out of marble, wood, or shiny brass. The book on the altar is called a sacramentary. The priest uses the prayers and blessings in the sacramentary to celebrate Mass with the congregation.

FLOWERS: People in the church volunteer to decorate the altar with beautiful flowers. Flowers remind us of life and of the beauty of God's creation.

CANDLES: The candles in church are there to remind God's people that they, like Jesus, are to be a light to the world.

LAMB OF GOD: The symbol on the lectern is of the Lamb of God. The Lamb of God is a title used for Jesus. The Lamb is carrying a banner, which means that Jesus is risen from the tomb and is victorious over death.

CREDENCE TABLE: The table near the altar, where the cruets that hold the wine and water, the basin, and the finger towel are placed for the priest to use during Mass.

Some churches have beautiful pictures painted on the walls. Others have colorful stained glass windows or banners. Many of the pictures and windows show scenes from the Bible. In earlier times, many people did not know how to read. Instead, they could look at the paintings and stained glass windows and see the stories from the Bible. The images are another way of telling stories to God's people.

STAINED GLASS WINDOWS: These colorful windows show scenes of Jesus as a young boy and a young man.

Music as Prayer

ALL GOOD CELEBRATIONS HAVE MUSIC! We have music in church, too. Singing songs together in church is another way of praying to God.

The people who lead the congregation in song are called a choir. Some churches have choirs whose members are all children. Singing songs and playing musical instruments are wonderful ways to give thanks and praise to God.

ORGAN: A musical instrument played in many churches to lead the congregation in song.

At some special Masses, the priest will sing parts of the service and the congregation will sing other parts. Everyone follows the words and music in the books provided in the pews. At other Masses, the whole congregation sings along with the choir. Sometimes one singer will sing alone, accompanied by musical instruments. You might hear a piano, guitars, violins, trumpets, or even drums!

The organ is a popular musical instrument that is played in many churches. Some organs have large pipes that make beautiful sounds. Most organs can be found in the choir loft. The choir loft is like a balcony where the musicians and singers gather. Sometimes musicians and singers gather in the front of the church to lead the people in song.

PIPES: Long, tubular metal rods that are part of most organs. The pipes make beautiful sounds from the notes being played on the organ's keyboard.

BAPTISMAL FONT: A stone, metal, or wood basin where people are baptized. Some fonts are as small as a sink, and others are as large as a bathtub. The font is often located near the front door of the church, under the choir loft, or in a special place called a baptistry.

Sharing the Eucharist

WHEN WE GATHER WITH FAMILY AND FRIENDS for special occasions, we often share a meal together. When Catholics gather in church, they share a meal called the Eucharist, or Holy Communion.

The bread and wine that we use as food and drink are carried to the altar by people from the congregation, often a whole family. After the priest consecrates the bread and wine, they become for us the Body and Blood of Jesus Christ.

When we have special visitors for a meal, we often bring out our best glasses, silverware, and plates. When we celebrate the Eucharist, we use a beautiful cup called a chalice. Many chalices are made out of shiny silver or gold. Some have sparkling jewels on them. The

CRUETS: Small glass bottles holding the water and wine that are consecrated during Mass.

BLESSED SACRAMENT: The name used for the hosts after they are consecrated during Mass. They are the Body of Jesus Christ.

wine and some water from the cruets are poured into the chalice, and then with special prayers they are consecrated by the priest. The bread that is consecrated is placed on a special plate called a paten. It is usually made of gold or silver, like the chalice. The round, flat, white piece of bread that is placed on the paten is called a host. We believe that the host becomes the Body of Jesus Christ when it is consecrated.

The people come up to the front of the church to receive the host during Holy Communion. After eating the consecrated host, we feel that Jesus is even more present in our daily lives.

Offering Our Gifts

WE ALL KNOW THAT IT IS BETTER TO GIVE than to receive! The people of God support the church in many ways. They share their time by coming to church to pray and by volunteering for church activities. They share their talents by singing, reading, decorating, teaching, painting, landscaping, or playing musical instruments. And they make donations to help keep the work of the church alive.

During Mass, a collection basket is passed around the congregation so that people can make an offering to the church. This money is used to pay the church's bills. It is also used to fund programs that help people in the church. The money supports the religious education of children and helps other people in many ways. By offering our time, talent, and treasure, we show that we are part of a community that loves and serves others.

Often churches will have another place for donations, called a poor box, where we can give money to help those in need. The envelopes and coin slots near the votive candles are also used for donations. Many churches also have a box for gifts of food, especially around holiday times. We are all part of God's family, and we feel good when we share our blessings.

OFFERING ENVELOPES: Many people put their donations in special envelopes for the offering at church.

VOTIVE CANDLES: Candles that are lit in front of a statue of Jesus, Mary, or one of the saints. We kneel and light the candle to show that we are praying to them, requesting their help, and giving them honor. People offer money when they light candles to show thanks to God.

STATUES: Figures of Jesus, Mary, or the saints that are made of marble, stone, wood, plaster, or metal. Statues are found in almost all Catholic churches, and they remind us to pray for the help of the holy men and women who now are with God in heaven.

Preparing for Christmas

IT'S FUN TO PREPARE FOR CHRISTMAS! We bake goodies, decorate trees and houses, and shop for Christmas presents. In the Catholic Church, we prepare for Christmas during a season called Advent. The word *Advent* means "coming." During Advent, we remember Jesus' coming among us as a baby two thousand years ago. We also prepare for the time when Jesus will come again in glory.

During the four weeks before Christmas, we light candles on a circle of evergreen branches called an Advent wreath. The Advent wreath has three purple candles and one pink candle on it. Each week, we light a different candle and say special prayers.

The third Sunday of Advent is called Gaudete Sunday. *Gaudete* is a Latin word meaning "rejoice." We light the pink candle on Gaudete Sunday because we are joyful that the birth of Jesus is near.

The Advent wreath reminds us to prepare for the celebration of Christmas, when Jesus, the Light of the World, was born in Bethlehem.

WHITE CANDLE: Many churches place a white candle in the center of the Advent wreath on Christmas Day. This shows us that the waiting time of Advent is over, and Jesus, the Light of the World, is born.

PINK CANDLE: The candle that is lit on Gaudete Sunday, when we rejoice because the birth of Jesus is near.

MARY, THE MOTHER OF JESUS: This bright and colorful stained glass window shows Mary, the mother of Jesus. The angel Gabriel told her that she was going to give birth to a special baby. Mary then waited for Jesus, the Son of God, to be born. The image of Mary on this window is known as Our Lady of Guadalupe. In it, Mary wears a cloak of stars and heavenly blue.

Christmas Celebration

DECEMBER 25TH IS CHRISTMAS DAY, one of the most important holy days in the Catholic Church. This is the day when we celebrate the birth of Jesus.

Every Catholic church sets up a Nativity scene for the Christmas season. A Nativity scene shows the place where Jesus was born and the people and animals who were there. Jesus was born in a stable, a place where animals live. His crib was a manger, which is a box where animals feed. St. Francis of Assisi, who lived during the Middle Ages, started the tradition of the Nativity scene. He used real people and real animals. Today, some churches still have a Living Nativity. They use farm animals, and members of the church play the parts of the people who were there. But most churches use painted statues to create the Nativity scene.

The people standing near Jesus' manger are Mary, his mother, and Joseph, her husband. The angel in the sky announced the birth of Jesus to shepherds. They came to the stable with their sheep. The Wise Men were kings from the East who

HOLY FAMILY: Most churches use painted statues to create the Nativity scene. The people standing near Jesus' manger are Mary, his mother, and Joseph, her husband. We often call them the Holy Family.

WREATH: A circular arrangement of evergreen branches. Christmas wreaths are hung in churches to remind us that Jesus was born to bring us eternal life.

HYMNBOOKS: Books containing songs that we sing during Mass. At Christmas time, we sing Christmas carols to celebrate the birth of Jesus.

POINSETTIAS: Plants that were brought from Mexico in the 1800s. The Mexican people called them "flowers of the blessed night" because their leaves looked like the star of Bethlehem.

followed the star above the baby Jesus. They traveled on their camels to bring Jesus gifts.

The beautiful red plants that we often see in church at Christmas time are poinsettias. Their leaves remind people of the star that shone in the sky over Bethlehem, the town where Jesus was born.

The Christmas trees behind the altar are decorated with lights that help brighten the church. They remind us that Jesus is the Light of the World.

The Journey to Easter

"**TURN AWAY FROM SIN** and be faithful to the Gospel." The priest says these words on Ash Wednesday. He makes the sign of the cross on each person's forehead, using blessed ashes. The ashes remind us to do penance for our sins.

Ash Wednesday is the first day of Lent, which is the Catholic Church's season of prayer and penance before Easter. It lasts for forty days.

During Lent, Catholics make personal sacrifices to prepare for the celebration of Easter. Some give up things they enjoy, such as sweets or television. Catholics who are fourteen and older give up eating meat on Fridays and usually have fish instead. Some people also make extra-special efforts, such as saving money for hungry children or praying more often.

STATIONS OF THE CROSS: Images along the walls of the church where people stop to pray and think about the sufferings of Jesus and his Resurrection into eternal life.

HOLY MEN AND WOMEN OF NORTH AMERICA: These stained glass windows show the saints and blessed people who lived and worked in North America.

SECOND STATION OF THE CROSS: This beautifully carved, traditional marble station shows Jesus taking up his cross and beginning his journey to Calvary.

Following the Stations of the Cross is a wonderful way to pray during Lent. The Stations of the Cross on the church walls show fourteen scenes from the last day of Jesus' life. People stop in front of each station to say special prayers. The stations begin with Jesus being condemned to die by Pontius Pilate. They follow Jesus as he

carries his cross to Calvary, where he was nailed to the cross, and they end with Jesus being laid in the tomb.

The season of Lent ends with Holy Week. During this final week before Easter, we prayerfully remember Jesus' Last Supper on Holy Thursday and his death on the cross on Good Friday.

Rejoicing at Easter

"JESUS CHRIST IS RISEN TODAY, ALLELUIA!" These words from a popular hymn tell why Christians are so happy on Easter Sunday. We believe that Jesus rose from the dead and lives forever. We also believe that we are called to live forever with Jesus in heaven. Easter Sunday is the holiest and most important day of the whole year in the Catholic Church.

During the forty days of Lent, many churches display a large wooden cross in memory of Jesus' suffering and death. At Easter, the cross is draped with a white cloth. It reminds us that the white shroud that Jesus was buried in was found in his empty tomb on Easter Sunday morning. It is a sign to us that Jesus is alive.

The church's celebration of Jesus' Resurrection begins with the Easter Vigil service on Holy Saturday night. During this beautiful liturgy we bless our Easter fire, light our Paschal (Easter) Candle, and listen to God's Word. We also bless our Easter water, baptize and receive people into the Church, and share Holy Communion.

The church is always beautifully decorated with sweet-smelling, brightly colored flowers during the Easter season. The Easter fire, water, and flowers all remind us that life is a gift from God that lasts forever.

RISEN CHRIST: This carved wood statue shows Jesus after his Resurrection, overcoming suffering and death.

EASTER WATER: This jar contains the water blessed during the Easter Vigil. It is blessed by dipping the Paschal (Easter) Candle into it three times. The Easter water is used to remind us of our baptism.

LILIES: These beautiful white flowers decorate our churches at Easter time. They resemble a trumpet blaring out the good news that Jesus is risen from the dead.

CROWN OF THORNS: The sharp, painful crown that the Roman soldiers made Jesus wear as they mocked him.

Baptism into the Church

"I BAPTIZE YOU in the name of the Father, and of the Son, and of the Holy Spirit." With these words, a person is welcomed into the Christian community. In the sacrament of Baptism, we are washed clean of all sin. We are also reborn to everlasting life in Jesus Christ.

Our parents and godparents gather around the baptismal font as we are baptized. Godparents are special people chosen by our parents for us. Their role is to be good examples to us in living our Christian faith.

The baptismal font is a beautifully ornamented basin where the sacrament of Baptism is celebrated. It is usually made of stone, metal, or wood. The baptismal font holds the water that is blessed and poured over the person being baptized. Some churches have fonts large enough for children or adults to stand in. Babies usually are held by their parents as the water is gently poured over their foreheads.

The Paschal Candle that is blessed during the Easter Vigil service stands near the baptismal font. A small baptismal candle is lit from the Paschal Candle and given to the newly baptized person. It is a reminder that he or she is always to walk as a child of the Light.

HOLY WATER FONT: The bowl near the doors of the church that holds the blessed water. When we enter or leave the church, we dip our fingers into the font and make the sign of the cross. This reminds us of our Baptism. In some churches, the baptismal font is also near the front door.

The Oils of Gladness

IN THE CATHOLIC CHURCH, holy oils are used in the celebration of some sacraments. During Baptism, Confirmation, Holy Orders, and the Anointing of the Sick, people are anointed ("made holy") with oil. Certain objects such as altars, chalices, and patens are also anointed with oil.

There are three kinds of holy oil, called the "Oil of Catechumens," the "Oil of the Sick," and "Holy Chrism." The first two are made from olive oil. Holy Chrism is made from a mixture of olive oil and balsam. Balsam is a sweet-smelling liquid that comes from certain trees.

In Catholic churches, the holy oils are kept in an ambry. The ambry is like a chest or cabinet and is usually located on a wall in the sanctuary. Some ambries have glass doors so we can see the holy oils inside. Holy oils are used to remind us that the people of God are called to be holy.

The sanctuary also contains the Tabernacle. The Tabernacle holds the Blessed Sacrament, the host that was consecrated by the priest at Mass. When we visit a church, we usually stop in front of the Tabernacle to say a prayer to God.

SANCTUARY LAMP: A wax candle that burns all day and all night wherever the Blessed Sacrament is kept in the church. The candle is usually placed in a red container. The sanctuary lamp reminds us that Jesus is truly present in the Eucharist.

TABERNACLE: The box that contains the Blessed Sacrament. Tabernacles are usually made of gold or other metal, marble, wood, or stone.

HOLY CHRISM: The sacred oil called Holy Chrism is poured from the glass bottle into a small container for use. The priest or bishop dips his thumb into the oil when he anoints people or religious items.

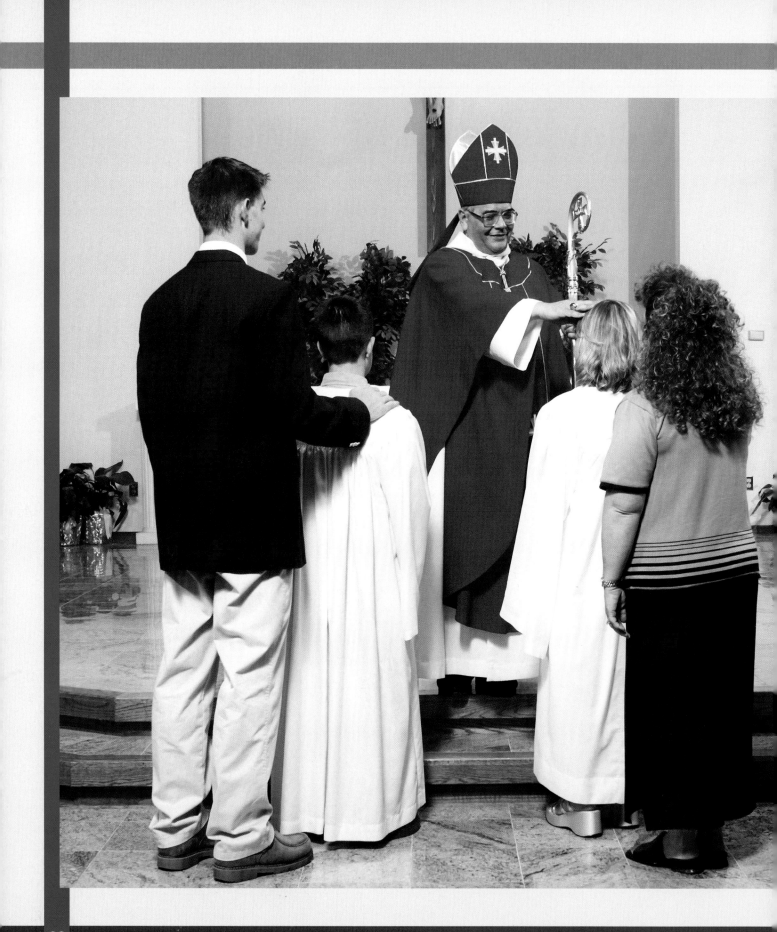

The Gift of the Holy Spirit

CONFIRMATION MEANS "TO BE STRENGTHENED." In the sacrament of Confirmation, baptized Catholics are strengthened by the Holy Spirit to become witnesses to their faith. Part of growing up is becoming strong in your beliefs, so Confirmation is celebrated when a child or young person is prepared to make that commitment.

During the Confirmation ceremony, the bishop or priest prays to God the Father that the Holy Spirit will be poured out upon those receiving the sacrament. He then extends his hands over those being confirmed as a sign of the coming of the Spirit. He then traces a cross on the person's forehead using Holy Chrism and says, "Be sealed with the Gift of the Holy Spirit."

When receiving the sacrament of Confirmation, the person is allowed to choose a new name. Some choose the name of a saint or someone who is very special to them. They may also choose a sponsor, who stands by the person being confirmed. The sponsor represents the community of faith who welcome and pray for the people being confirmed.

In Confirmation, a person accepts the responsibility of living and witnessing to the Christian faith.

BISHOP: A bishop is a priest who is ordained to follow in the footsteps of the Apostles. He is the shepherd of the priests and of God's people in his local area, called a diocese.

EPISCOPAL RING: A ring worn by the bishop as a sign of his commitment to the church.

MITER: The large folding cap that is worn only by a bishop. Miters are usually made of silk or linen and have beautiful designs embroidered on them.

CROSIER: A long staff that is carried by a bishop. It is shaped like a shepherd's crook, or stick, and represents the bishop's role as shepherd of his flock.

Behind the Scenes

ALMOST ALL HOUSES HAVE A ROOM where people store decorations, clothes, and other items. Churches also have a special room where items used during religious ceremonies are kept. This room is called a sacristy.

The sacristy has closets where the priest's vestments are hung. Vestments are colored robes with beautiful designs that are worn by the priest during Mass. Green, white, purple, and red are the colors of the vestments most commonly worn in the Catholic Church. Priests wear white vestments during the seasons of Easter and Christmas, purple ones during Lent and Advent, and green ones during the ordinary time of year. Red is used on Palm Sunday, Good Friday, and the Feast of Pentecost. The priests say special prayers as they put on their vestments.

Many sacristies have handsome cabinets where religious items are kept. Chalices, patens, altar wine, altar bread, lectionaries, and sacramentaries are all put in the sacristy for safekeeping. The beautiful cloths that are used to cover the altar are also stored in big drawers in the sacristy.

The sacristy is also the place where altar servers put on their robes and prepare to help with the celebration of the Eucharist.

CHASUBLE: The outer garment worn by the priest during Mass. In the Catholic Church, the chasubles are green, white, purple, and red. Chasubles are usually made of silk, velvet, or other fine material and are decorated with religious symbols.

STOLE: A liturgical vestment that is worn around the neck of the priest. It is long and thin and matches the color and material of the chasuble.

SACRAMENTARY: The book of prayers and blessings from which the priest reads at Mass.

About SkyLight Paths

SkyLight Paths is creating a place where children and adults of different spiritual traditions come together for challenge and inspiration, a place where we can help each other understand the mystery that lies at the heart of our existence.

SkyLight Paths creates beautiful books for believers and seekers of any age, a community that increasingly transcends the traditional boundaries of religion and denomination—people wanting to learn from each other, walking together, finding the way.